Reflections on Reality

Monica Greer

BookLeaf Publishing

Presentation by *BookLeaf Publishing*

Web: www.bookleafpub.com

E-mail: info@bookleafpub.com

ISBN: 9789357213189

First edition 2023

Sacrificial Awareness

What do you do with the knowledge you can't
share

Knowledge you've held, carried, labored to
destroy though it lives so you care

You care to share it but it's not permitted so its
overstayed it's welcome in your hearts lair

So you watch others equipped with this truth
poison the ignorant with their lies

So I ask again, what do you do with the
knowledge that screams behind your wanting
eyes

Eyes that can barely make out a view from the
cries

Am I so unwise as to surmise that I can carry on
much longer in this disguise

Sizing up every occasion as the unfit & soon to
be the last time

Time that I will get to hug her, see her stand or
even hear her soft tone

I tell you, I cannot bear to just have these
moments simply via phone

That is a tow away zone for it will easily lift
away a part of my heart with a force to emit the
saddest groan

We cannot maintain in this state of the insane,
for how can another hoard the pleasure of time
or on it place a strain

The more, the added, the "extra" we feign for,
the glorious endeavor of what we want to gain,
the more

But I see now, the venom of her matriarch has
begun its erosion

Have you ever wandered what can cause a
families implosion?

Division or even altering the mind of one's decision, oh yes it's no specific situation it's simply called manipulation

So you work with pride to get paid the lies that you bake as melodic truth & to her you feed

And she eats what you provide, drinks from the thoughts that it's only you she will ever need

Sadness wells within a fellow daughter who wouldn't know the makings of a man without her own father

So you my fellow so called mother, you were robbed of a gift of a daddy, let alone a man to be your father

You turned that misdemeanor into your felony of having your daughters true fatherly bond be of no bother

A bother, perhaps, a nuisance an occurrence that you stand to keep minimum

Deleting for her a history, a legacy of beautiful people, part of where she's from

So I ask you again, what do I do with the knowledge, the reasons, the facts that have led us to this hollow ground

Ive swam with the waves of hurt, floated with the rising tides of reality, drifted to where I feel I am no longer earthbound

I've resolved that all I have left is to wade in the waters of this knowledge to then lie breathless, into it I've drowned.

Sabotage

Sabotage, sabotage, sabotage
Enraged at the engaged minds that are bonded, apprehended, imprisoned with pride
Pride… circled around the lions mane, the lions main components
Though even his opponents, opposing thus deterrent to its blood
It's kind, it's natural intake to fully induce one to abdicate, abdicate any said authority, ignoring with sheer ignorance any seniority
Trumping love with rabid hate, openly rabid, foaming within its rabidly infected core, overflowing into its every move, deciding on a whim with no evidence
No reason for succession to probe, yes sabotage, the ideal seems surreal
But the fate as of late in view seems skewed, lewd imaginations of
Unfulfilled prophesied revelations, this wreaks of the feces that wallows below the step of each trek in this sabotage,
Your sought out win to simply lose, your tired, dreadful mirage
The oasis you saw just to be the inferno that cauterized

Your pupil, sabotage, sabotage, sabotage, driving
away your ego to trade in for foolishness
Only to settle for reason to let it rot in the
garage, sabotage, you dullard saboteur, you
never succeed and yet you always want more.

More Than Just Sorry

Let me begin to apologize for those who may feel ostracized at my opinion…
or perhaps unapologetically skip approach to straight forgiven,
forgiven for the accompaniment of my misery,
please pardon her uninvited presence that now clouds your scenery,
you see, she doesn't care for the sorry or apologies, no see it's annoying like the pimples you tweeze,
or the mascara you drown your eyes in for that man you want to please,
it's unwanted, unwarranted, even it's sound is a tease,
not one of sought out pleasure, not desired, no not in any measure,
see a "sorry" was once created, and or meant to be manual, it was a term of its own origin,
then it was plagiarized, for the automatic to set in,

now, see now, the "sorry" is a go-to, quick release, a scapegoat, you stub a thought, break a soul, "sorry", now you gloat,
ah yes, you've found the hole in the boat, will that piece of tape keep you afloat,
you can deliver a speech yet miss the keynote,
sometimes sorry isn't good enough, it barely scratches the surface, and before your gloried ego does resurface...
the trance, that trance had you in belief you dissolved a need, the rash reached sepsis, the exposure of its depth has you inclined to plead,
see now is when you want details, now you see the tilt in compassion on your scales,
instant gear shift to a facetious view, only to result in your anger, in your ineffectiveness you stew, fixated on the fixation that "sorry" is sufficient, but how can heat be released without a vent,
my soul is burning, being charred and scarred with each ember of life's flame,
eyes that will hear and ears that will listen to what I proclaim,
sample on my opinions, dine with my thoughts, feast upon my feelings, drink my insecurities, please, take my body within your arms, squeeze, drain my entire being with your embrace, lift up my spirits and carry me over this hurtle in my

race, place my feet upon a path, a new start, at my pace,
see, don't settle for "sorry", don't lean upon a bargained plea,
agree to attempt, agree to open the vent, and hold the robotic responses in contempt,
for each time can be meant for more, no matter the time, rhyme or reason before,
leave the sorry at the door, silence is not your enemy and your heart is your mentor,
yes, a core full of effort gives much to restore.

Reluctant Acceptance

Is this what stupid feels like
Is my indiscretion openly exposed in my very expression
Should I continue with further utterances or allow this to be my lesson, shall I graduate with lonely to accept my career in emptiness, for surely my masquerade with acceptance and obsession with feelings has me a mess, am I truly unable to be satisfied, should I accept the surface or superficial, just accept the fact it was tried, they say to be true to yourself but I keep placing my truth on the shelf, for you, for the yearning within, for your truth, I'm aging with passion and dying in loves youth, I want you, but I realize we can't always have what we want or even desire, I do know that I can't offer my heart up to anyone, it's not up for hire, the location was entered as you for my final destination, if though I am for you a burden or a tiring obligation, I'll drag my feet and regrettably leave to unease your vexation, I can't promise I'll forget you, for I'll never love again,

you are the lyrics, the tune in my hearts
pulsation, I could beg but I won't force
negotiation, you have your space now,
nonetheless still the star of my admiration, I'm
sorry, I'm sorry my love was heavy or excessive,
spread your wings my nonpareil and live.

Our Song

Below are my lessons, lessons learned, lessons continued…learning, yearning to sit upon your frontal gaze earning the granted lift in each new phase,
pace, pace myself so as to take in every main fact, certainly I want to make an impact, in no way though detract, from you my educator, your edification I adore
a loquacious belle I am indeed, oozing with attraction sprinkled with gratitude I bleed, drifting into a daydream, my eyes you misread, I guarantee I've learned well, your expectations I'll exceed
I osculate my lips upon your chin, slower & lower I go agitating the veins upon your neck, my hands graze the soft hairs that rise with each peck, she wants to unleash yet she keeps her desires in check
I procure a soft melody, perhaps an ode to your allurement, staring at your skin isn't enough I much touch, I must feel, I must breathe in your copious scent
the way your hands glide across my inner thigh deadens my fear, your palms flow against my mid back, your fingers trickle my hips,

trepidation leaves its station & insecurities are
nowhere near
the torrent has made cracks in her veneer, every
time you pull me closer, each breath you make
upon my ear, the surge rises, the cascade is here
you stroke the drops of my libido, as your
majesty stands before me below, my hands cup
your hips ever so gently, as if precious cargo,
yes, my dear, I am ready, I lead, you follow
raise me atop your throne so that I may extol
you in dance, lift, swirl, fast to slow, all
hedonism does enhance, our eyes tightly shut,
but our souls are in a trance
our bodies change course and you indulge me,
total fulfillment, all mortality, you may have
conquered the waves but you have not tamed the
sea
see, a want, a desire may be able to be satisfied,
with you, I am never content, more is never lied,
too much is a myth, to be replaced, opposite of
your side I don't want to be with,
you serenade me with your voice, you calm me
with every touch, you know all my pressure
points, my every fervor is in your clutch
you taught me to love, to love myself, I'm still
learning, knowing you seek this, keeps my heart
burning
we climax together providing utter delight, I
melt into the puddles of your pupils within my

eyesight, this is that feeling, the feeling that all is alright, this must be the definition of the good, in goodnight
you have truly silenced me, peacefully, the humility of your nature, the modesty even in its subtlety, it truly sets us apart, sets us free
perhaps this is love unconditional, love as it should be…
I learn from you, you absorb from me…
Sorry for staring my dear, in you, in this I'm deeply invested, you softly snore, the soothing sounds of hearing you rested,
Feeling my place, my whole being is you revitalize, the melody remains in my mind of how our bodies did harmonize,
do you hear it my love, the sweet tune, so strong…?
yes, yes that is our song.

Cheek to Cheek

Cheek to cheek I sought to have with you & I
seek the cheek that melts against mine,
pleasure ensues with each time he takes to lay
his upon mine,
intertwine our love, for it is different, would
neither sell nor rent it…to anyone, less one, be it
had to be, his dad to see the same, feel the love
yet not as ours, cannot be compared , shared ,
bared by even the strongest of men,
yet within he and I it is heavy,
like the nine months of a uterus weight carried
thru, rubbed my belly until I saw it to be true,
I had an embryo growing, thriving within my
soul, I thought I was whole until now, I thought I
held true to words until this vow, vow of
complete trust, to thrust aside ambitions,
traditions, I have an omission of pride
nonetheless my mission lies inside of me, to not
just "be all I can be", but do all I can do,
reach heights higher than before, ignore the
forethought of failure, seduce the adventure and
make love to all it brings, learn the music of thy
instrument and flirt with it's strings…
I've never felt love like this before, a mother I
am, no wonder this time, no scam,

I'm drawn to his face and captured by the touch
of his hand, I wake up to a smile, trial in my day
then his day end smile is my okay, my okay to
push thru, endure, defeat what tries to defeat me,
so my son can know despite the feat,
I will complete all task assigned with a smile on
my face and a love all mine, he deserves that, all
facts shown he is owed that…
my beautiful boy, decked with brown hair, each
inch of his body air brushed with beauty,
truthfully did he come from me?
I see his father in his reflection, Jehovah made
no mistakes in this construction of him,
constructing each centimeter of cuteness, i
assume this is why I love him so, his daddy's
blood runs in his veins this his glow,
it shows so clearly, oh how I love him so dearly,
oh there's that smile, that's my kryptonite, my
cup of good coffee, my morning delight, the
sight of him, nothing sweeter then the rest as he
sleeps upon my chest, only to awaken to those
almond eyes that embarrass the skies,
the eyes that break my heart whenever a tear
falls from his cries, here I am my son! Mama is
here, come close, I'm always near, whenever
your in doubt don't fear, mama is listening,
enlisting for your request for me, I will run to
you, to have you here with me, because I sought

for something I still seek, you & I forever cheek to cheek.

- A poem dedicated to my beautiful son Christopher Scott Greer Jr.

Live to See

Can you promise forever?

Can hope be a quest for the lost?

Will an “x” mark the goal in this endeavor?

Or is it beyond redemption, a non refundable cost?

Standing in a frozen zone, with the soles of each foot numb,

unaware of the shattered psyche to the sudden outcome.

Can you promise forever?

Can that fear within, yes, her fear, can you sever?

Sever it, destroy it, can you even know it?

The particles that crystallize her tears,

or the thunder from each beat her heart bears,

the palpitations with no variations but deep
hollow thrusts,

so an empty vow, stitched with romantic thread,
she may not trust.

Model this new style of weathered adornment,

align her neck with the pearls of consent,

for she has no other jewels of real value,

the cubics, rhinestones, they carry no kilo true.

The rusted rings, corroded chains, leave her
unsure

As her pupils sparkle at the ruby you dangle, it's
authenticity you assure,

You assure her of such, notarized with the
softness in your tone,

Coupled with the quick look, gliding eyes,
unrealized groan,

Perhaps a distant intentional response to the
blinded masses,

The minority that resides within her takes note
as each of your pawns passes

Her mind is racing, debating temporary and or
final transition

Repetition is her ol' reliable, now, though she
reaches for suspicion

Dangerous tool, stored for years, corroded,
lacking power

Her fingers drop despair, so behind doubt she
will cower

The alarm sound echoes announcing the lonely
hour

Levitating during duties due to its wondering
power

Over and over thinking, can one really promise
forever

Promise that forever will be the home we
possess,

Or shall my love be foreclosed and earths soil
my address

Can you promise me forever?

Can you promise me sole access to your heart?

Can you promise me an end to never?

Can you promise me a part?

A part to the link that connects me with you,

No, rather that binds me, adhesively, with no breakthrough,

Live the forever, be the forever, now, tomorrow, perpetually,

Nurture the dirt of what you commit, harvest the ground of hope you want me to see.

Do you believe that of which you tell me in advance?

May your utterances not be for the sake of romance

My margin for error in this regard is zero,

No mood for outstanding attempts of grand gestures, no, not a quixotic hero,

Genuine, baring each flaw of your vascular core,

So you promise me forever? Well I still want more,

Never I did, for I do, yes, I do, it is my rapport,

Can you, can you promise me forevermore?

Any less and I'm slain, nothing to live for.

Love Sick

Yearning, yes I yearn, to discern your deepest thoughts , I've sought for the emotions that lie deepest in your core, therefore the deprivation I suffer leaves my soul sore, I want you ever, ever more

To caress the supple skin that laces your bones, to be locked within your embrace, the lane in your eyes with no passing zones, I moan, I moan loudly with my heart erupting sweet pleasure from my lips, goosebumps arise upon my skin as your hands slide to my hips

I am yours, unequivocally, I bask in your handsomeness embodied in all your masculinity, you my dear are apart of me, I crash into you and you dive into my sea, you see, it's depth that is beneath us there is no limit, there is only one size and you are my right fit

Your heartbeats tune I have on steady repeat, I've been held captive by your look at the very moment we did meet, you are my gravitational pull, my five course meal of which I am never full

I am undeniably bound to your love, even time apart you're all I think of, some may think I'm blind, obsessed, insane too, all I know is my heart belongs always, incessantly to you.

Equanimity

Everybody wants to be heard within the words they unfurl as an arrow to a target , but at large yet is just the amount of shards that, the bullets left behind that left one in charge to disengage to disarm to then reach for the calm, that was not before the storm that thundered ever so loudly are we then proudly or proud we, have eaten our counterparts fear or fear their lightening rebuttal in this weathered struggle of who is right or wrong or be gone, for reason that a settlement is too far gone or a settle is meant for the forlorn, so be it exit now to stage left for they won't give up their crown, glistening with its prideful golden glow just to rust like a cosmetic jewel, a value they'd not know lest they burn their metallic core to refine to just subject to human and be kind to rewind the object personalities to them, cancel formalities and all the why didn't we see, see where that thought missed your not and all the stops given simple forethought, to realize we are sending equal forget me nots, taste the recipe that was built not for I but we to cash out the wins when we yank on those slots to then dine on the fight for true love, fill our intestines with endurance blessings and create a

dessert most only dream of, the battle is not for the weak at heart , the thread that copies the rubber band and tear apart, rather stretch each love ligament, don't allow a little swelling to disrupt your dwelling, even while tears are welling, within your eye to assume things a lie or say things not meant, each be a manner in which the arrow is sent, landing
on the mark of contentment, speak to be spoken a countless many occasions to vent, better to outline then ferment, descent as a team into the pit marked repent, carry on to be resilient in and on the battle present, consent to admit that even imperfection looks good in content.

Virtue of a Woman

It is the truest virtue of a woman, real women speak, words & terms some bleak yet leak all fluid emotionless yet no less emotion is suppressed within that beating organ in her chest, lest I say I am one, a woman, one of realism, a prism of beauty through expression, a lesson to some men, even most women, who think it's ok to not cry, shy away from the admit & deny, denial of an action, immaturities reaction, seen in the hidden, no I must say that it's forbidden to my heart to hide, feelings must show, I have to swim with the tide or id drown in what is a lie, at truth I could not look in the eye, for I, I was being the otherwise not wise, being what is common, far from a true woman, a typical, cynical girl, trapped and wrapped up in all chosen, a choice in a game, straight losing, no that's not me, don't let it be you, I wear all I feel, undress what I won't conceal, you'll never carry a wonder, but you'll ponder on my somethin', that's my virtue, I'm a true woman.

What do I do?

Roses are red, violets can be blue, tulips can be pink, lilies can showcase in all colors unique. You came ashore , I sailed the sea, you scouted few, I hid from many. Yet you jumped into the shallow, swimming swiftly to the deep, now floating beneath my eyes, do I jump to my demise? Do I risk the swim to shore? You outstretch your hand, then belief filled me more. Wet with fear and facing the unseen, our bodies float to sand, passing the unknown in between. A Melody arises so we stand to dance, dare I question, or just take the chance...

Jaded

Expectations are simply a self induced elevation
of a level in a game, no one wants this played
situation,
Pons of puns indeed intended to uproot the roots
of a liaison upended,
Dependent on the depended thought of need,
Subjected to the false perception shackled in a
prison called greed,
Sentenced to months or years to life not right but
write how alls alright,
Right or wrong it's left to right the wrong of the
place love does belong,
Voicing the notes as a ballad when it's clearly a
different song,
Filing the feeling of the fiction to a genre that is
authored upon a new dictation,
Mishap perhaps during progressional cessation,
elated to be masqueraded by the jaded view that
thoughts or feelings ever mattered to you.

Worth the Worth

Each inward outlook of herself was another twist
of her plastic heart

the wrinkles that fossiled seem to now be her
work of art

why cant she just do more then see, rather
believe that with her lies value

that even with every self-inflicted twist everyone
can still see through

see through the muddled pieces that only she
can't get past

the onerous trust that her worth is vast.

What do you see?

If you scatter all the pieces,

rectify the

cuts and changes, yet leave no

traces...seal the tattered

corner to garner favor and yet

thru all such labor, it will

never be the same, shame, for

shame it is for what is

reality without the real? Where

can you relate if you cannot

first feel...

to feel is to what, to when, to find...

To what would you say for sight to blind

To hear regarding the deaf to ring forth
memories to mind

Divine entrance into the ability truly would land
the hopeful in tranquility

Really we would want nothing less for the more
to have that chance

To be beheld as full or complete per chance at
first glance

For our hand to bow against another in this
adjured dance

Self

Drafted into the infantry of
solidarity,
crashing
within the walls of
of
despondencies
parody,
the only makeup she ever wore
most
suitably,
dutifully
surrendering to what
she
surmises
as
her
fate,
fatally ignoring the self induced
weight.

Zuri

I've been introduced to embryonic moments and
to tailored meets

This tiny human has unearthed an additive to
shame all sweets

Her opals pigment secretes a dense liquid that
cling to yours as a lodestone

All consciousness at loss when within her aura
now in a twilight zone

Blown away by the stature to length in its tiniest
form

Formulating your words proves as futile to cool
your emotions when they're this warm

Even the most stellar swimmer would be
engulfed at her pukka vocals

A vice grip of her petite knuckles would humble
the strongest of nobles

It's as if the art of Swahili sketched her name
solely for her

Truly that curve of her soft hair to the winning
smile, beautiful as that definition I concur

For sure my sweet kitten you are beautiful,

filling the heart sacks beyond the bagful

At a time of loss, your precious soul brought you
through the crack in my heart

Now having surpassed a days time I never ever
want to be apart

In part, it could spark my dear Zuri,

purely the saddest fury,

Surely with tears in absence I'd miss the fever
that you healed

I remain thankful to be your aunt, to care for you
whenever possible, to protect, to shield

You are a gem, perhaps marking the completion
to an unrivaled rivière

Gratitude I bestow to you for my breath was halted until I inhaled your air.

•Poem dedicated to my 6 month old Niece- Zuri Greer

Unsolved

Neglected & disrespected, different definitely
and contradicted

Contract addicted to the notarized fiction

Exposed and imposed upon to expedite eviction

Slow turn, yielding to easy pleasure

Chased and lost upon in every inch in measure

Random thoughts entering this jagged prism

Flaws, cons, faults in all you cannot list them

Peer into the pupils peep hole

Squinting to find the half to your whole

Filtered unfiltered atoms in each part

Severed the thread stitched to the bleeding heart.

Bruit

What's that sound? Do you hear it?
I've told you, she's told you, even he
Who's the source, can it be all three?

Whiplash from the swift neck turns to hear,
Waiting for the next note in fear,
Like that same cooked meal
Or the fractured film on the reel,
You've taken a vice grip on the rim of ears
wheel

With the faint odor of admiration
But all the scents are incense fumes of
desperation,
Are the many sayings that go far in any and
every way,
Yet you miss the direction, the signs pointing to
hearsay

The sound is loud, as that dirge on repeat,
A tune never unsung but always on beat,
So we bop our heads and tap our feet,
Feeding the forces that only want our defeat

That apple tree is producing sure, will the rotten be that of your prime choosin'?
Our ears hear all, but of every word, will you listen?

This is the melody of all
The he said and she said,
But they said, what's in your head?

Sing your song, cook your meal
Place the film on your minds reel,
Cast the hearsay, bring back real.

Caption This…

If you had no clue
And solution was solved on a whim of whatever felt new..
If every given fact was a guess, a destination a simple small swipe of a wipe in the largest mess...
Would you address the location with the latitude to proper longitude with tact
Respect the boundaries unkept to erect the signs that lack
Buckling the belt to ensure stability in the seat pressed upon your back
Steering parallel with pretentious rails completely off track
Tagging hash-heartedly in your disparity
Aiming for a share, a tap twice over for clarity
Forced upon recognition is the saddest of charity…
Chair the standing weary heart to elevate its channels for streaming
Subscribe your mind to silence to enjoy this trial on dreaming.

Compulsive

Six, five, four, three, two, one...
One more moment, just one more day,
One more hour, one more way,
To find that one more minute, begin to end but it didn't end in limit, limiting oneself, obsolete, incomplete, one to you, two for truth, three odd to do, a full measure dealt to true, four stories even, time left stagnant for the rise to leaven, leaven the grain by five, elevated to a whole new high, equalize my mind, psychotic perception to hysteria in line, count the account and account for each, beseech the obsessive to control to decide, careless to be for to care less was tried.

Recipe

Rushing, step by step, no slowing down
No break, Awake! To the vision, open eyes into
this, succulent sweet bliss
Blissful rain of suckling drops as soft bullets,
Alter the view, changing your every move,
losing choice in what to do..breathe!
Inhale, exhale, in and out, in and out…
Bouts of deep exhale, blushing at my thoughts
that impale, shards pierced my heart straight
through, this is what I feel for you,
Rubbing my hands to saturate them,
Pulling off the garment to it's final bend in this
road of pleasure far from its end,
And just then…I whisper I love you, as the kiss
leaves you to land upon my lips, like pellets of
dew, "twas then unknown became no less then
what I knew, you and I began to collide in one
notion, my knuckle swiftly swivels you to focus
on this motion, slow & steady as you descend
into my ocean, I'm
open for you have me alive, destined for this
destination into each other we arrive, heart unto
heart we thrive, deep breaths in sync with our
moans our bodies cave in, the assurance as I
brush against your skin you're my haven, those

hands that hold me just right, never loose & tight
enough to never let go, yet I let go head to toe,
I'm yours, mind, body and soul, let's go slow,
watch our wet bodies glow, levitating us above,
stirring all that is our recipe, making love.

www.ingramcontent.com/pod-product-compliance
Lightning Source LLC
Chambersburg PA
CBHW051745130826
49812CB00033B/1009
9789357213189